1/27/10

Sports and My Body

Cycling

Charlotte Guillain

Heinemann Library
Chicago, Illinois

www.heinemannraintree.com
Visit our website to find out
more information about
Heinemann-Raintree books.

To order:

☎ Phone 888-454-2279

💻 Visit www.heinemannraintree.com
to browse our catalog and order online.

© 2009 Raintree
an imprint of Capstone Global Library, LLC
Chicago, Illinois

Customer Service: 888-454-2279

Visit our website at www.heinemannraintree.com

Edited by Siân Smith, Rebecca Rissman, and
  Charlotte Guillain
Designed by Joanna Hinton-Malivoire
Picture research by Ruth Blair
Production by Duncan Gilbert

Originated by Raintree
Printed and bound in China by South China Printing
Company Ltd

13 12 11 10 09
10 9 8 7 6 5 4 3 2 1

**Library of Congress Cataloging-in-Publication
Data**
Guillain, Charlotte.
  Cycling / Charlotte Guillain.
    p. cm. -- (Sports and my body)
  Includes bibliographical references and index.
  ISBN 978-1-4329-3457-6 (hc) -- ISBN 978-1-4329-
3462-0 (pb) 1. Cycling--Juvenile literature. I. Title.
  GV1043.5.G85 2008
  796.6--dc22
                                   2009007085

Acknowledgments
The author and publishers are grateful to the following
for permission to reproduce copyright material: Alamy
pp. **11** (© Jenny Matthews), **17** (© Seb Rogers); Corbis
pp. **5** (Wolfgang Rattay/Reuters), **10** (Sean Justice), **13**
(Hill Street Studios/Stock This Way), **16** (Ariel Skelley),
21 (moodboard); Getty Images p. **15** (David McNew);
iStockphoto pp. **18**, **22**, **20** (© Pathathai Chungyam),
22 (© David H. Lewis), **22** (© Craig Barhorst), **22**
(© Michal Kolosowski); Photolibrary pp. **6**, **7**, **8**, **9**, **12**,
14, **19**, **23**, **23**, **23**, **23**, **23**, **23**; Photoshot p. **4**
(Liang Qiang/Xinhua).

Cover photograph of boys riding bicycles reproduced
with permission of Getty Images/Sean Murphy/Lifesize.
Back cover images reproduced with permission of
iStockphoto: 1. bicycle pump (© Michal Kolosowski);
2. helmet (© David H. Lewis).

Every effort has been made to contact copyright holders
of material reproduced in this book. Any omissions will
be rectified in subsequent printings if notice is given to
the publishers.

Contents

What Is Cycling?.....................4

How Do I Learn to Cycle? 6

How Do I Use My Legs and Feet? 8

How Do I Use My Arms and Hands?. . 10

What Happens to My Body When
      I Cycle? 12

Why Do We Cycle? 14

How Do I Stay Safe Cycling? 16

How Do I Take Care of My Bicycle? . . 18

Does Cycling Make Me Healthy? 20

Cycling Equipment..................22

Glossary 23

Index............................24

Find Out More 24

Some words are shown in bold, **like this**. You can find them in the glossary on page 23.

What Is Cycling?

When we ride a bicycle, we are cycling.
Cycling is a type of exercise.

People cycle as a sport or to get
to places. We can also cycle for fun.

How Do I Learn to Cycle?

training wheel

Many people learn to ride a bicycle with **training wheels**. They help you to **balance** as you learn to ride.

When you are ready, you can take off the training wheels. Then you learn to balance and **pedal** at the same time.

How Do I Use My Legs and Feet?

You use your legs to hold the bicycle still on the ground. To start moving you put one foot on the ground and push a **pedal** forward with the other foot.

You use your legs and feet to pedal and
move the bicycle. You can pedal fast
or slow.

How Do I Use My Arms and Hands?

brake

You use your hands to hold the handlebars and steer the bicycle. You might use your hands to ring a bell or use the **brakes**.

You can use your arms to show other people where you are going.

What Happens to My Body When I Cycle?

When you cycle your heart starts to beat faster. You may feel hot and sweaty.

leg muscle

When you cycle fast you will breathe more quickly. The **muscles** in your legs will start to feel tired.

Why Do We Cycle?

When you cycle you can travel farther and faster than when you walk. You can visit new places.

It is fun to cycle with friends. Everyone can learn to cycle.

How Do I Stay Safe Cycling?

A teacher can tell you how to cycle safely. It is important to wear a helmet when you are cycling.

If you are cycling in the evening, always use lights. You should also wear light-colored clothes that drivers can see easily.

How Do I Take Care of My Bicycle?

Keep your bicycle out of the rain when you are not using it. You might also use a bicycle lock to keep it safe.

tire

Make sure your **brakes** are working properly. Always check to see that your **tires** are pumped up.

Does Cycling Make Me Healthy?

Cycling is good exercise and will help to keep you fit. You should also eat healthy food and drink plenty of water.

To stay healthy you need to get plenty of sleep. Then you can have fun in many different ways.

Cycling Equipment

helmet

light

lock

pump

Glossary

balance keep yourself or an object steady so that it does not fall

brakes parts of a bicycle that you use to slow the bicycle down or stop it from moving

muscle part of your body that helps you to move. Exercise can make muscles bigger and stronger.

pedal part of a bicycle that you push with your foot to make the bicycle move. When you use pedals to make something move it is called pedaling.

tire thick rubber ring that covers the edge of a wheel. Tires are usually filled with air.

training wheels two extra wheels attached to either side of a bicycle to make it balanced, or steady

Index

balance 6, 7, 23

brakes 10, 19, 23

equipment 22

exercise 4, 20

helmet 16, 22

learn 6, 7, 15

lights 17, 22

lock 18, 22

pedal 7, 8, 9, 23

pump 19, 22

safety 16, 17, 18

steer 10

tire 19, 23

training wheels
6, 7, 23

Find Out More

www.nhtsa.dot.gov/people/injury/pedbimot/bike/
KidsandBikeSafetyWeb/
This Website has some great safety tips.

http://kidshealth.org/kid/watch/out/bike-safety.html
On this Website, you can learn which hand signals you
should use when cycling.